GW00599595

HANDCUFFS

AND OTHER RESTRAINTS

A BRIEF HISTORY AND SURVEY

****

ALEX R NICHOLS BA(Hons)

To Keith with best wishes from Alex

1

CONTENTS.

1. INTRODUCTION.   p. 3.

2. HANDCUFFS (MANACLES).   p. 8.

3. LEG-IRONS (FETTERS).   p.11.

4. GRIPS ETC.   p.13.

5. MISCELLANEOUS RESTRAINTS.   p.15.

6. CONCLUSION.   p.17.

7. BIBLIOGRAPHY.   p.19.

8. ILLUSTRATIONS.   p.21.

2

1. INTRODUCTION.

It seems highly likely that human beings have been using restraints upon each other from the earliest times. When it was discovered how to make cord and rope from grasses and reeds, or to cut rawhide thongs from the hides of animals, these materials were probably used as restraints. Indeed, it may be argued that part of the process of civilisation entailed the immobilisation of individuals by the use of restraints rather than killing or maiming them. It is known that Neanderthal man made ropes and these could have been used for restraint. The body of the man found in the peat bog at Tollund showed marks of a plaited cord around his neck, though it is not clear if this was as a restraint. The earliest writings make reference to the taking and binding of prisoners, either in warfare or for slaves. From early times art has shown the binding of prisoners, for example, Assyrian bas-reliefs on display in the British Museum show many scenes of bound prisoners-of-war. Some of these reliefs show bonds that appear to be square contraptions, which could be wood or metal rather than cord or rope. It is certain that these materials were used for restraints, wooden stocks and pillories and metal artifacts can still be seen in many places. Ancient literature abounds with accounts of chaining, the Bible, for example, has accounts of restraints made of brass and iron.

Metal became the preferred material for security and long term use, first copper, brass and bronze, then iron. Metal presented a problem because chain could not be securely knotted like rope. Methods of fastening had to be devised. Before the lock was invented, rivetting was probably the usual form of fastening, though sometimes soldering or welding was employed. A simple fastening could be devised by hammering shut an open iron or brass ring. Iron restraints, in the form of slave gang chains and manacles have been found at several Iron Age sites in Britain and mainland Europe. In Roman times, quite sophisticated locks were made, judging by the evidence of keys found at many sites and manacles were made that had locks, but these were not common (Fig.1). Roman manacle locks were usually of the spring wedge lock type (though of a different

3

design to that shown in the diagram). This type of lock has a mechanism consisting of two parts, a plunger in the form of a double spring which makes a wedge when open and a tube, into which the plunger is pushed, engaging a projection in it which prevents its withdrawal. The key is a device that squeezes the spring wedge flat (Fig.2).

In medieval times also there were lockable restraints, but these were very much the exception. These locks were often of quite complicated construction, either integral to the restraint or separate padlocks. None-the-less, **at all times until the eighteenth century, hammered rings and rivetting were by far and away the most common methods of fastening** (Fig.3). Such restraints were removed by opening the rings or breaking the rivets with a hammer and cold chisel, hence the expression that irons were "struck off".

Ordinary, everyday articles were adapted for use as restraints. The most obvious example is the nautical shackle, the U shaped metal gadget used to secure rigging on a ship. Two of these threaded onto a metal bar produce a very effective restraint called the bilboes (Fig.4) and may well be the origin of our common use of the word shackles to describe restraints in general. (A fine example can be seen on board HMS Victory at Portsmouth). The origin of modern restraints is probably based upon bilboes and the development of locking mechanisms for them.

The spring wedge lock survived for a very long time and is typical of the pre-industrial revolution individual blacksmiths' work. This lock usually turns up in the form of restraints known as "slave irons" (Fig.5). These are usually of leg-iron size, rarely handcuffs. There are two shackles, only one of which has a spring wedge lock, the other is locked by threading the connecting chain through an enlarged link, a device of ancient origin, present in the Iron Age restraints alluded to earlier. Most of these restraints are said to be of Middle Eastern origin.

By the eighteenth century, the barrel lock had become common.This consists of a tube in one half of a hinged shackle containing a plunger, at one end of which there is a projection which engages a hole in the other

4

half of the shackle. This plunger can be withdrawn from the hole by screwing in a key on the opposite threaded end, usually against a spring, thus releasing the lock (Fig.6). A common version of this type of lock was the "Dutch" padlock, which was still offered in a manufacturer's catalogue in the 1950s.

The barrel lock restraint became the universal type, popularly known as "darbies" (Fig.7) and from the middle of the eighteenth century these were manufactured in large numbers. As the industrial revolution began in England, it is not surprising that British manufacturers proliferated. One firm founded in 1780, Hiatt's of Birmingham, is still in existence and is one of the world's foremost handcuff makers; its products are the ones most likely to be seen in British Commonwealth countries. Britain's position as a colonial power and above all its major role in the slave trade, provided ample markets for the restraint makers. Hiatt's were still offering "nigger collars" in their catalogue at the end of the nineteenth century (Fig.8).

However, it was in ex-British colonies, the United States of America, that the first advances on the barrel lock patterns occurred. In 1860 W.V.Adams patented an adjustable handcuff that became the prototype of a wide range of handcuff types available in the U.S.A., some of which inevitably travelled abroad (Fig.9). Most commonly used were the types invented by E.D.Bean (Fig.10) and J.J.Tower (Fig.11), but there were many other kinds as designers tried to produce ever more secure and easily usable models. This experimentation culminated in the "swinging bow" type invented by G.A.Carney in 1912 (Fig.12) and since then almost all modern handcuffs have been variants of that basic design.

In the latter half of the twentieth century, plastics became common substitutes for metal in many fields. It is not surprising therefore, to find that plastic restraints are common. The type most usually seen is the "plasticuff", a restraint consisting of a band of strong plastic, like that often used by gardeners as a plant tie. This has a simple non-keyed lock at one end, through which the other end can be threaded, ratchet serrations engaging and preventing the end from being withdrawn;

5

release is by cutting the band (Fig.13). Adaptation for use as handcuffs is easy and some plasticuffs are even made so that the lock can be opened with a standard handcuff key and some with a press-button release or modified locking mechanisms, for training purposes (the latter brightly coloured to avoid use with real prisoners!).

Strong polypropylene webbing has also been utilised, usually in conjunction with a type of fastening that uses hook and loop material popularly known as "Velcro", its first manufacturer's trade mark. Hand and leg cuffs, arm restraints and belts are made for use not only in the penal field, but also for violent patients in hospitals (Fig.14). Standard swinging bow type handcuffs have been made almost entirely from plastics because of the concern about the transmission of H.I.V. These handcuffs are capable of being sterilised in an autoclave if contaminated by prisoners' body fluids.

Canvas and leather are often used to make restraints. Straps, with or without locking buckles, and straitjackets are made. Such restraints were mostly used in hospitals on insane patients. Leather belts of various designs are also used as supplementary restraints. For example, it is common in the U.S.A. for a belt, fitted with a D-ring in the middle, to be put on a prisoner's waist, buckled at the back, with a pair of handcuffs threaded through the D-ring in the front (Fig.15).

The belt restraint presents one solution to the problem of the transportation of dangerous prisoners, which has become a matter of increasing concern in recent times. Various types of restraint chains and handcuff covers have been invented, along with various kinds of combination sets. These have been designed to maximise the restriction of prisoners. The simplest is the combination set consisting of a pair of handcuffs and a pair of leg-irons, joined together by a length of chain (Fig.16). More complex is the security cover, a device that fits over a pair of handcuffs after they have been applied, covering the key holes and then secured with a waist chain (Fig.17). Then there are various kinds of gang chain whereby a number of prisoners may be secured together. These devices seem to hark back to the "coffle" of slave trading days;

that was a device, often wooden, that secured two or more slaves together by the neck (Fig.18). The modern devices link the prisoners by their handcuffs.

Another type of restraint is the **grip**. These are sometimes seen in museums, or illustrated in books, incorrectly called handcuffs, but they are quite different. A grip always requires the captor to hold onto it as a means of maintaining control of a prisoner and is never lockable. It is, in effect, a strong extension of the captor's hand. Such devices have been in use at least since the seventeenth century. A simple grip consisting of a leather thong about 20cms long with a wooden toggle at each end, has been described in use in Italy in the mid 1600s (Fig.19). This was twisted about the prisoner's wrist and the toggles held by the captor, who could tighten his grip by twisting it if his prisoner showed signs of resistance. This type of grip is still being manufactured, though made of chain. A more complicated pattern is the scissors type. One half of a figure eight shaped gadget is placed over a prisoner's wrist and the other half is used as a handle by the captor, secured by a spring clip (Fig.20).

The use of restraints as a means of preventing the escape of prisoners is obvious, but another function seems to be that of making sure that prisoners **are identified as such, to themselves and for all to see!** One training manual describes handcuffing as a symbolic act and it is common in many countries for people to be automatically handcuffed on arrest, even in situations where escape is not a consideration. Another example is the recently reintroduced chain gang of the U.S.A., where it seems that the function of the restraints is mainly to humiliate. That too was the major function of the pillory and stocks of olden times.

Restraints of various kinds have been used by people throughout recorded history and, almost certainly, for a very long time before. In modern times, after the industrial revolution and the advent of machine tools and mass production, restraints have become very sophisticated. **This history of restraints is only about the devices manufactured in an organised manner since then.** Those made before the industrial revolution were by comparison, primitive makeshifts.

7

2. HANDCUFFS (MANACLES).

For a very long time the standard handcuff pattern was that popularly known as "darbies". These are generally lockable with a spring-loaded barrel lock, though some are made that require the locking plunger in the lock to be screwed down. This is especially so with the type known as "plug eights" (Fig.21). After the plunger is screwed down in the lock, the keyhole is sealed by screwing in a metal plug, using the top end of the complicated key. These are also made in the standard two shackles joined by a chain configuration, as well as the more usual solid eight shape illustrated. All these handcuffs are non-adjustable, but are available in several different sizes to accommodate variable wrist sizes. This is of no use to the constable on the beat and so an adjustable type, the "Scotland Yard" pattern was introduced in about 1880 (Fig.22). This pattern is adjustable to fit a wide range of wrist sizes. These and the ordinary darbies are still being made by Hiatts and remain very much in use, particularly in under-developed countries.

In 1860, in the United States of America, W.V.Adams patented an adjustable handcuff with a distinctive shape, but without specifying how it should be locked (Fig.9). The basic design was developed by John Tower with sophisticated locks patented in 1878, 1879 and 1882 (Fig.11). This type of handcuff is often seen in Western films, even in those which purport to tell stories about events long before those dates! The last model is a very secure handcuff indeed, the lock is much more complicated than the simple barrel lock and has a double locking facility. After the handcuff is placed on a prisoner's wrist, the key is inserted in the lock and given a turn in the opposite direction to that required to open it. This operates a mechanism which prevents the locking catch from withdrawing, so that the handcuff cannot be further tightened. This makes picking the lock much more difficult, especially by the method known as "shimming", which requires a very thin piece of metal to be inserted into the lockcase, between the ratchets and catch, which would open the shackle.

In 1882 Edward Bean invented a type of handcuff that was very popular

(Fig.10). The swinging arm is made so that it is entirely enclosed in the lockcase when the shackle is shut. It will not lock in that position though, until a thumbknob is depressed which releases the locking bolt. These handcuffs are not as secure as the Tower models and cannot be double locked. Both types, in common with nearly all other kinds of handcuff of the time, suffer from the fact that they can be deactivated by a resisting prisoner. Such a prisoner simply shuts the handcuffs before they are applied to the wrists, leaving the hapless captor having to unlock them again before they can be used.

In 1912 George A.Carney invented a handcuff of a revolutionary pattern. His design was of a shackle that had a "swinging bow". The ratchet part of the shackle rotates a complete 360° and goes through the lockcase in such a way that it will not lock unless there is a limb in it. He did not specify a particular locking mechanism, but various people have invented suitable locks. Almost all modern handcuffs are variants of this pattern, commonly known as the "Peerless" type after the name of the company which first made them commercially. The standard pattern has a chain linkage (Fig.12), but hinged (Fig.23) and solid designs are now frequently seen. British police nowadays often use a solid design known as the "Speedcuff" (Fig.24).

The Peerless pattern is also popular with its users because it can be "flicked" onto a prisoner's wrist and is adjustable to most sizes. There is a standard size, but several firms supply a range of larger sizes. For example, Hiatt's De Luxe range handcuffs are 15% larger than standard. The larger firms sell leg-irons with short chain linkage that can also be used as large handcuffs (Figure 33). Almost all models are capable of double locking, usually by means of a peg on the top of the key, which is used to depress a plunger in the lock mechanism. This immobilises the catch that engages the ratchet teeth, so that the shackle cannot be further tightened. Besides making the handcuff more secure, this reduces the risk of injury to the prisoner. Perhaps the strongest and best made handcuff of this type is the "Super" or "F.B.I." model made by Harrington and Richardson until 1951 (Figure 25). Production ceased because it was expensive compared with Peerless or Smith & Wesson models.

9

The observant person will note that nearly all modern Peerless type handcuffs have similar keys, so that one key will open all such handcuffs regardless of manufacturer. Several firms even make "universal" keys, somewhat larger than the standard key, which are easier to use. The locks can be picked quite easily, which is why the makers specify that handcuffed prisoners should not be left unattended. This problem has been tackled by making more sophisticated keyways, the Pouta handcuffs (Fig.26), for example, have a more secure keying system. The most extreme example is the Chubb "Escort" handcuff (Fig.27) which looks like a pair of extra secure padlocks. This is probably the most secure handcuff in current use and is much favoured by the Prison Service. Special inserts are provided to increase the range of small sizes. One of the neatest and easiest to use designs is that of the Australian "Saf-Lok" pattern (Fig.28), which has a complex key to operate a cylinder lock through the double locking button. This handcuff cannot be unlocked unless it has been double locked.

Another solution to the security problem is shown in the French Rivolier handcuffs (Fig.29). There the double lock is activated by a separate cylinder lock, so that two keys are required to open the handcuffs when double locked. When not double locked, they operate as ordinary Peerless type handcuffs, though the key is somewhat larger than usual.

Special handcuffs are made by several manufacturers for a variety of purposes. A pair attached to a leading chain, for example, or a pair fitted with a longer than usual chain linkage. Perhaps the most unusual example is the range of heavyweight handcuffs produced by the German maker Clejuso, the heaviest of which weighs a massive 1.3 kilograms (Fig.30).

It is interesting to note that very often the makers of handcuffs are also the manufacturers of guns. This is particularly so in the U.S.A., where Colt, Harrington & Richardson, Iver Johnson and Smith & Wesson are among the best known. In Europe, for example, the French gun makers Manurhin have also made handcuffs and the Bren company of the Czech Republic make the "Pouta" brand restraints (Fig.26).

3. LEG-IRONS (FETTERS).

As restraints for the hands are made, so are those for the feet. These are usually larger versions of handcuffs. As there are darbies for the hands, so there are darbies for the feet, larger, of course, and usually with a longer chain linkage (Fig.31). Sometimes the linkage is by a bar rather than chain, this was said to be popular in the British Colonial Service. It is usual for leg-irons to be of much heavier construction than handcuffs. All the British ones of this pattern seem to be of a standard single size, only varying in the length of the chain linkage. This is sometimes very long, two metres, for example, with perhaps a large ring in the middle for attaching to handcuffs or a wall. Sometimes a single leg-iron attached to a single handcuff, or a range of combinations is seen, but more of that later. Abroad, a range of darbies variants is made. In Germany, Clejuso made an adjustable leg-iron rather like a large "Scotland Yard" pattern handcuff until about 1980 (Fig.32).

Not surprisingly, the Peerless pattern has been adapted for use as leg-irons by being made about 50% larger. There is little variation, the vast majority of designs look like a larger pair of ordinary Peerless handcuffs, though with a longer chain linkage, usually about 30cm. However some are made with a distinctly different shape, Smith & Wesson for example, (Fig.33). This different shape is claimed by the makers to be a more secure fit and is also a slightly larger size than the norm.

In Germany, Clejuso make a leg-iron of a pattern somewhat reminiscent of the Bean design (Fig.34). These are not of the swinging bow pattern and are considerably heavier in construction, in common with their generally heavier handcuffs. The French manufacturer, Rivolier has recently produced a leg-iron that seems to be a "throwback" design, in that it is non-adjustable and is locked with a simple screw down bolt mechanism rather like a plugless "plug 8" (Fig.35).

Leg-irons are not used in Britain nowadays, indeed there is a positive aversion to their use here. It is illegal to manufacture or export them, though not to import them. Abroad, there is no such ban and they are much used. The most notorious use, perhaps, is in the U.S.A., in the chain gangs that have recently been reintroduced there. There the shackles have been made with much longer linkage chains than normal so that prisoners are linked and can move about to work. Each prisoner wears two pairs, one on each leg with the other shackle of each pair attached to a different fellow prisoner.

The stocks at Painswick in Gloucestershire. These show what seems to be a transitional stage between medieval wooden stocks and modern leg-irons.

4. GRIPS.

Grips have been in use from the beginning of the modern period at least. The early Italian design with leather thong and wooden toggles was soon replicated in iron (Fig.36). These are commonly called "wrist crackers" or "twisters" and it easy to see why. When applied to a prisoner's wrist, they are firm and if any resistance is shown, the captor merely has to twist the chain to apply a painful reminder to comply. Sometimes these are used on a handcuffed prisoner, the chain twisted around the handcuff linkage so that more control can be gained by the captor. There are French designs that seem half way between these two types, they have wooden toggle handles, but instead of a leather thong, there is a chain made of wire spring links.

In this country, the standard grip has been the scissors pattern (Fig.20) sometimes called "snips". When closed on a prisoner's wrist, the grip is held shut by a spring clip in the handle, covered by the captor's hand. This is the type so frequently, wrongly, described as handcuffs, though they were developed from an early attempt to make a scissors type handcuff in the mid 1800s. These are particularly effective when used on a prisoner's arm, twisted up behind the back. Manufacture ceased in Britain in about 1980, but this and the previous type are still made by Clejuso in Germany.

In the U.S.A., in 1869, W.Gray Phillips invented a grip (more usually called a "come-along" by the Americans) which he called a "nipper" (Fig.37). Several variants of this design were made, including one where the closure was activated by a trigger, so that the grip siezed the prisoner's wrist as soon as it touched it. Some were of a simple hook pattern, with a hinged bar closure held shut by the hand of the captor.

Some grips are of complicated design, like those known as "claw" grips. One modern design, made in Taiwan (Fig.38), has to be placed over the prisoner's wrist and the handle turned until the grip is tight enough and then a knurled nut is screwed down to secure it all. There is a German design (Fig.39), that has a complicated spring loaded action. These types

13

have been in common use, particularly abroad, for some considerable time. As always, most experimentation on these devices has been in the U.S.A. and many designs have been patented there, but never commercially produced. Some devices were invented that could be converted into handcuffs if needed, but these never caught on, mainly because they were so complicated. This made them costly to produce and tricky to use.

There is a restraint closely related to the grip, a kind of hybrid, sometimes called a cabriolet, which usually has one ordinary Peerless type shackle attached to some sort of handle. These often look as though someone has taken away one T-piece handle from a chain "wrist cracker" grip and replaced it with a shackle. Most seem to be of French manufacture. There is a marked resemblance to the restraints referred to later in the Miscellaneous section, where sometimes pairs of handcuffs are made attached to varying lengths of chain. There is an American pattern that has a single Peerless type shackle attached to one end of a 1.5m. length of chain with a 10cms. diameter ring for a handle at the other end (Fig.40). This seems to be very much the type of restraint that is designed primarily **to make prisoners know that they are prisoners and to demonstrate that fact to others,** rather than prevent escape.

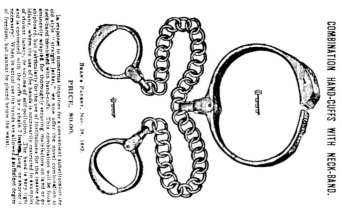

Illustration from an old catalogue of about 1890 of a Bean collar and handcuffs.

5. MISCELLANEOUS RESTRAINTS.

Reference has already been made to the fact that restraints are sometimes used in combinations and they are often used with supplementary equipment. Well known from earlier times is the "ball & chain", offered by one maker in the U.S.A. in the late 1800s in weights varying from ten to fifty pounds, attached to single or double leg-irons. A typical example of the combination usage is the Clejuso set referred to earlier (Fig.16). This allows a prisoner to walk, sit, eat, drink and use the toilet, all things necessary if a prisoner is to be transported for a long distance. One version of this restraint in the U.S.A., called by its manufacturer the "auto restraint" (Fig.41), is specifically designed for use when transporting a prisoner by car (automobile in American parlance), presumably over a relatively short distance. All the chains are shorter than usual, but designed so that the prisoner can walk, albeit with difficulty, even get into a car, but cannot run or attack the guard.

Another solution to the problem of handcuffing a prisoner so that the guard is safe from attack and yet the prisoner can sit reasonably comfortably and perform simple functions, is the belly chain. This is a waist chain with handcuffs and is commonly used in prisons in the U.S.A. (Fig.42). It restrains the prisoner by chaining the hands at the sides. When leg-irons are used as well, this is quite a secure combination. In Marion top security prison in the U.S.A. a prisoner is not allowed to leave a cell unless so secured (see back cover picture). Various kinds of belt have also been in common use for some time. The Prison Service in this country have used a very strong leather belt, fitted with handcuffs on each side (Fig.43). In the U.S.A. various kinds of leather belts and harnesses are in use, some lockable. Recently the RIPP company there has produced a range of belts made from strong polypropylene webbing, with "Velcro" fastening. They vary from a simple belt with a D-ring (Fig.44), to a type almost identical to the Prison Service one, but with Peerless type handcuffs.

Various types of plastic handcuffs have been referred to earlier, but double versions of the plasticuffs are made (Fig.45) and these, as well as

15

the single ones are usable with a variety of belts. Even gang belts are made that can utilise plasticuffs and secure a number of prisoners together. It is more usual though, for groups of prisoners to be secured with gang chains. Sometimes these are chains with the handcuffs already fixed on them, like the pattern produced by Clejuso (Fig.46) and some times they are designed for use with the customer's own handcuffs. A chain made by C & S Security Inc. in the U.S.A. (Fig.47), comes in varying lengths and numbers of security links to suit the customer's requirements. It can accommodate ordinary or hinged handcuffs, or handcuffs fitted with a security cover.

Various kinds of leading chains are used, particularly in the U.S.A., the simplest consisting of a length of chain, about 1.5m., with a 10-15 cm. ring at one end and a 5cm. ring at the other. A pair of handcuffs can be threaded through the small ring and the large ring is used as a handle by the captor. Some makers supply leading chains with the handcuffs already fixed at the end, or in any combination to suit the customers' requirements.

The security cover or box consists of a hinged contraption made of very strong plastic, which is closed over a pair of ordinary chain linkage handcuffs. As a result the handcuffs resemble the "Speedcuff" type rigid shackles, but the keyhole is covered. Some have slots for double-locking, but usually the handcuffs have to be double locked before the cover is fitted. The cover is then locked in place by the belly chain's interlocking system and further security is added if the chain is also padlocked and the prisoner fitted with leg-irons (see back cover picture).

The jougs, collars and neck-cuffs were common in the medieval period, but in modern times such things were used almost exclusively in the slave trade (see Figures 8 & 18) and in African colonial territories. Early models had plug locks, but later the barrel lock was used. However, there was a Bean pattern collar, with attached handcuffs, on sale in the U.S.A. in the 1890s (see p.14) and a similar device was patented there by D.B.Rayburn in 1931. Such restraints are rarely used nowadays.

6. CONCLUSION.

Perhaps, as something of an afterthought, mention should be made of thumb and finger-cuffs. These seem to have developed from the medieval thumbscrew and finger-stocks. Various new types have been invented in modern times, but these have never caught on. They are not easy to apply safely so as to be escape proof, something which has made them popular with magicians. They have tended to be regarded as novelties and are frequently sold in joke and magic shops. However, their inventors meant them for serious use. The thumbcuff that turns up most often is a cheap, but well made pattern from Taiwan (Fig.48).

Many kinds of toy handcuffs have also been marketed over the years, early ones of the late 1930s made of metal and recent ones made of plastic as well as metal (Fig.49) can be found.

This brief history and survey of restraint equipment has, of necessity, only covered information about the mainstream of such things and then only the most common items. The range of types of restraint that have been used in the last two centuries or so is enormous. Since Adams first patented his idea, there have been hundreds of models patented in the U.S.A. alone. Indeed it seems that that country is the world's most restraint minded country. In August 1996, a convention of Correctional Facility staff there attracted over six hundred exhibitors to its trade stands, a large proportion of whom were marketing restraint equipment.

Literature on the subject of restraints is not readily available, especially for pre-medieval equipment. A list of material possessed by the author is appended, largely American and much of it out of print. Of this list, the Stanley Smyth Collection catalogue is very useful and has drawings of most of the handcuff types of the industrial West. Ian McColl's book is also very helpful because it contains well over a hundred of the inventors' original drawings. Hugh Thompson's article is essential for information about early restraints. First rate is Tom Gross's book with excellent photographs and a most informative text. Much useful information can also be found in manufacturers' and dealers' marketing literature.

17

The author has had access to various collections, including Europe's largest collection of restraint equipment, that of Chris Gower and also to a series of articles about handcuffs which he wrote for *Keyways*, the locksmiths' periodical. The author's collection of restraint equipment can be seen in the National Museum of Law at the Galleries of Justice in Nottingham.

Collections of restraint equipment can be seen at several other museums in this country, for example:-

London; The Clink Prison.
The London Dungeon.
The Tower of London.
Gloucester Prison Museum.
Inverary Jail.
Leicester City Museum.
Liverpool City Museum
Norwich Castle.
Stirling Old Town Jail.
Warwick Castle.
The Welsh National Folk Museum, St. Fagans Castle.
Winchcombe, Town Hall Museum (Simms Collection).
York Castle Prison Museum.

Single pieces are often on display in many places, for example there is a very fine pair of medieval restraints on show at Penhow Castle in Gwent.

7. BIBLIOGRAPHY.

Books, booklets and periodicals:
1. Andrews, William. *Old Time Punishments.* Dorset Press. 1991. (1890).
2. Anon. *Handcuffs, U.S., Vol.1.* Desert Publications. 1977.
3. Anon. *Torture & Punishment.*(The Tower of London). H.M.Stationery Office. 1975.
4. Barnard, B.G. *State of the Art Review, Handcuffs for Police Use.* Home Office. 1989.
5. Cannell, J.C. *The Secrets of Houdini.* Dover Books. 1973.
6. Clarke, A.A. *Police Uniform and Equipment.* Shire Publications. 1991.
7. Clede, Bill. *Police Non-Lethal Force Manual.* Stackpole Books. 1987.
8. Everett, Susanne. *History of Slavery.* Bison Group. 1978.
9. Gibson, Walter B. *The Original Houdini Scrapbook.* Corwen Stirling. 1976.
10. Gower, Chris. *Keyways.* April, June, August and October 1995. "Handcuffs - Their History and Development".
11. Gross, Thomas. *Manacles of the World.* 1997.
12. Held, Robert. *Inquisition.* Qua D'Arno. 1985.
13. McColl, Ian. *Handcuff Patents.* 1997.
14. Norman, Dick. *Locksmith Ledger Magazine.* February, April, May, September and October 1957. "Know Your Handcuffs".
15. Norman, Dick. *Handcuff Secrets for Magicians.* 1957.
16. Peters, John G. *Tactical Handcuffing.* Reliapon Inc. 1988.
17. Smith, Patterson. *The Gun Report.* (U.S.A.) March 1957. "Shackling Devices".
18. Stewart, Don, Ed. *The Stanley H.Smyth Collection.* Key Collectors International. 1981.
19. Thompson, Hugh. *Archaeological Journal 150.* p.57-168. "Iron Age And Roman Slave-shackles". 1993.
20. Wresch, Richard C. *The Houdini Collection, Niagara.* Catalogue. 1961

Manufacturers' marketing literature:-
1. U.K.   Chubb Safe Equipment Co.
              La Trobe Handcuffs Ltd.
              Hiatt & Co. Ltd. Several from about 1900-1996.
              Reuben Craddock & Sons Ltd. (Price list c.1955).
2. U.S.A.   American Handcuff Co.
              Bean. (Handcuffs and holsters) (c.1880).
              C & S Security Co. Inc. (Supplementary Equipment).
              Hiatt-Thompson, Inc. (American associate of Hiatt's).
              Humane Restraint Co. Inc. (1982 & 1997) (Mostly
              hospital restraints).
              Monadnock Inc. (Plasticuffs).
              Peerless Handcuff Co.
              RIPP Restraints Co. Inc. (Polypropylene and Velcro).
              Smith & Wesson Inc.
3. Germany. Clejuso. (Clemen & Jung, Solingen).
              Horst-Stein. (Moabit - Drawings only).
4. France.   Rivolier.
5. Spain.   Proselec Espana.
6. Australia. A.D.I. (Australian Defence Industries).

Dealers' catalogues:
1. U.K.   Fetters, London. (1992).
              Handcuffs International U.K. (1982).
              H.P.P.(U.K.) Ltd. (Trojan brand handcuffs).
2. U.S.A.   W.S.Darley & Co. (1996).
              S.A.French of New York. (1887).
              T.J.Ferrick. (Pre-1960).
              Patterson Smith. (Pre-1960).
              Reliapon Police Products. (1996).

8. ILLUSTRATIONS.

All items are from the author's collection, unless otherwise stated.
Scale indicates inches and centimetres.

1. Roman manacles (Hugh Thompson).
2. Diagram of a spring wedge lock.
3. Old leg-irons with rivet closure (HM Prison Service Museum).
4. Bilboes. (Chris Gower Collection).
5. "Slave Irons". (Chris Gower Collection).
6. Diagram of a barrel lock.
7. Hiatt "Regulation" darbies.
8. Page from an old Hiatt catalogue of about 1900.
9. Adams handcuffs. (Chris Gower Collection).
10.Bean Handcuffs.
11.Tower handcuffs.
12.Peerless handcuffs.
13.Plasticuffs.
14.RIPP quick-cuffs. (RIPP instruction leaflet).
15.Leather "D-ring" belt. (Humane Restraint catalogue).
16.Clejuso "Hamburger" combination set.
17.Hiatt "Blue Box" security cover and chain.
18.A coffle of slave trading days. (Illustration from a magazine).
19.Italian leather and wood grip.
20.Standard grips.
21."Plug Eight" handcuffs. (Chris Gower Collection).
22."Scotland Yard" pattern adjustable handcuffs.
23.American Handcuff Co. hinged handcuffs.
24.Hiatt "Speedcuffs".
25.Harrington & Richardson "Super" handcuffs.
26.Pouta handcuffs.
27.Chubb "Escort" handcuffs and inserts.
28.Australian Defence Industries "Saf-Lok" handcuffs.
29.Rivolier high security handcuffs.

32. Clejuso old pattern leg-irons.
33. Smith & Wesson leg-irons.
34. Clejuso new pattern leg-irons.
35. Rivolier leg-irons.
36. Clejuso steel chain grip.
37. Phillips "Nipper" grip.
38. Taiwanese "Claw" grip.
39. German "Claw" grip.
40. Hiatt-Thompson single shackle and leading chain.
41. American Handcuff Co. "Auto Restraint".
42. Smith & Wesson belly chain handcuffs.
43. Replica Prison Department restraint belt.
44. RIPP "D-ring" belt (RIPP catalogue).
45. Monadnock double plasticuffs.
46. Clejuso gang chain.
47. C & S Security Co. gang chain.
48. Taiwanese thumbcuffs.
49. Various toy handcuffs.

Page 12. The stocks at Painswick, Glos.
Page 14. Bean collar and cuffs (dealer's catalogue).

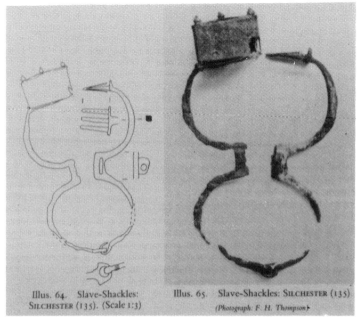

Illus. 64. Slave-Shackles: SILCHESTER (135). (Scale 1:3)

Illus. 65. Slave-Shackles: SILCHESTER (135)
(Photograph: F. H. Thompson)

Figure 1. Roman manacles. Illustration in *Archaeological Journal 150*. (Hugh Thompson).

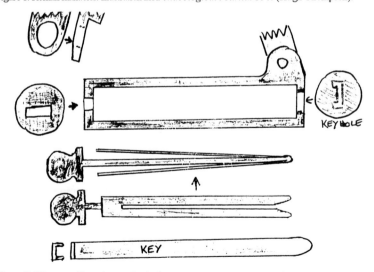

Figure 2. Diagram of a spring wedge lock.

23

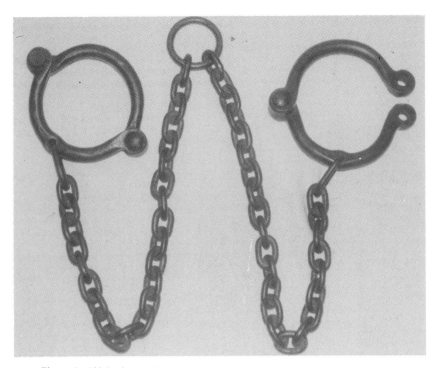

Figure 3. Old leg-irons with rivet closure. (HM Prison Service Museum [AAPSM 1990.0083], displayed at Gloucester Prison Museum).

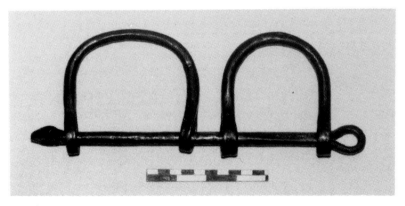

Figure 4. Bilboes. Lockable by a rivet or hammered ring in the hole in the end of the rod. (Chris Gower Collection).

24

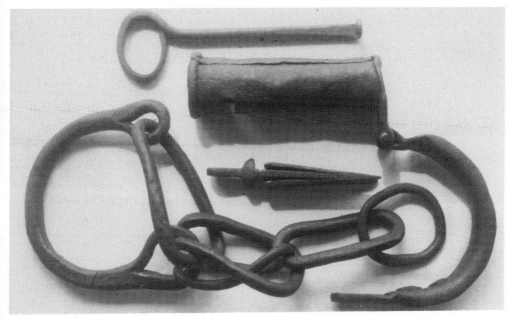

Figure 5. "Slave Irons". Although old and rusty, still in working order, with key. (C.G.Coll.).

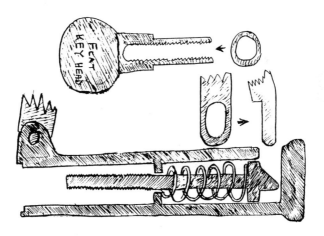

Figure 6. Diagram of a barrel lock.

Figure 7. Hiatt "Superintendant" model darbies.

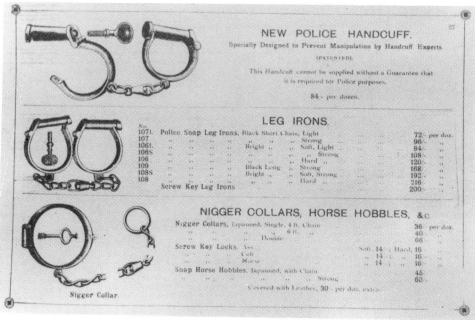

NEW POLICE HANDCUFF.

Specially Designed to Prevent Manipulation by Handcuff Experts

(PATENTED).

This Handcuff cannot be supplied without a Guarantee that
it is required for Police purposes.

84/- per dozen.

LEG IRONS.

No.								
107L	Police Snap Leg Irons. Black Short Chain, Light						72/-	per doz.
107	,,	,,	,,	,,	,, Strong		96/-	,,
106L	,,	,,	,,	Bright ,,	,, Soft, Light		84/-	,,
106S	,,	,,	,,	,,	,, Strong		108/-	,,
106	,,	,,	,,	,,	,, Hard ,,		120/-	,,
109	,,	,,	,,	Black Long ,,	Strong		168/-	,,
108S	,,	,,	,,	Bright ,,	,, Soft, Strong		192/-	,,
108	,,	,,	,,	,,	,, Hard ,,		216/-	,,
	Screw Key Leg Irons						200/-	,,

NIGGER COLLARS, HORSE HOBBLES, &c

Nigger Collars, Japanned, Single, 4 ft. Chain		36/-	per doz.
,, ,, ,, 6 ft. ,,		40/-	,,
,, ,, Double		66/-	,,
Screw Key Locks, Ass		Soft, 14/-; Hard, 16/-	
,, ,, Colt		,, 14/-; ,, 16/-	
,, ,, Horse		,, 14/-; ,, 16/-	
Snap Horse Hobbles, Japanned, with Chain		45/-	
,, ,, ,, ,, Strong		60/-	
Covered with Leather, 30/- per doz. extra.			

Nigger Collar

Figure 8. Page from an old Hiatt catalogue of about 1900.

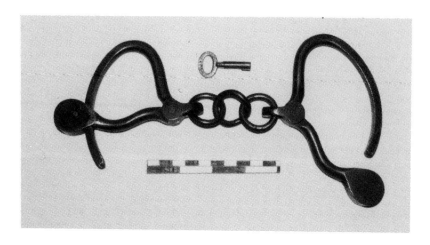

Figure 9. Adams Handcuffs. (C.G. Coll.).

Figure 10. Bean Handcuffs. Note the push button below the keyhole on the left hand shackle.

Figure 11. Tower Handcuffs.

Figure 12. Peerless Handcuffs. Model 300 pattern.

28

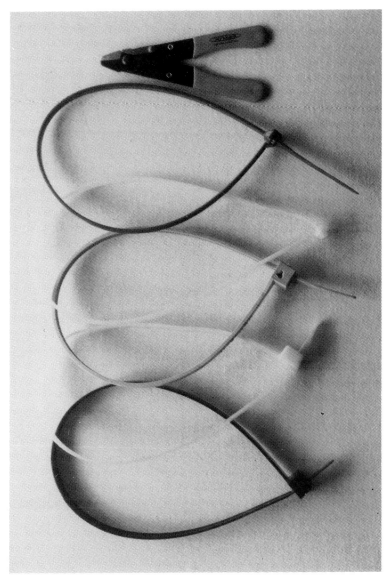

Figure 13. Plasticuffs, various makes (note the pattern with keyhole) and special cutter.

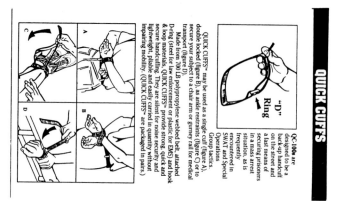

QUICK CUFFS

QC-100s are designed to be a back-up handcuff on the street and a fast means of securing prisoners in a mass arrest situation, as is frequently encountered in SWAT and Special Operations Group tactics.

QUICK CUFFS™ may be used as a single cuff (figure A), double locked (figure B), as ankle restraints (figure C) or to secure your subject to a chair arm or gurney rail for medical transport (figure D).

Made from 700 LB polypropylene webbed belt, attached D-ring (steel for law enforcement or plastic for EMS) and hook & loop materials, QUICK CUFFS™ provide strong, quick and secure handcuffing. They are silent for noise security and lightweight, pliable and easily carried in quantity without impairing mobility. (QUICK CUFFS™ are packaged in pairs)

"D" Ring

Figure 14. RIPP Quick-cuffs. Instructions leaflet.

HUMANE TRANSPORT BELT

Figure 15. Leather "D-ring" belt. Illustration from Humane Restraint catalogue.

Figure 16. Prisoner in the Clejuso model 128M "Hamburger" combination handcuff and leg-iron set.

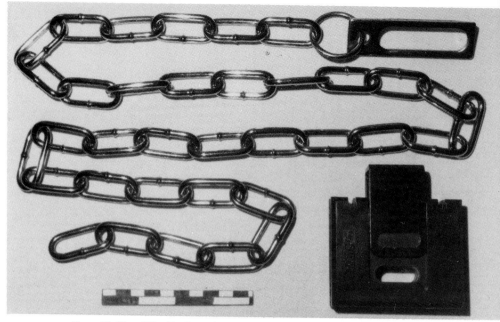

Figure 17. Hiatt "Blue Box" security cover and chain. (See also back cover picture).

Slaves travelled from the interior in coffles, linked together by iron collars and clinking chains. Some, like these, remained as chain-gangs at the coastal "factories."

Figure 18. A coffle of slave trading days. Illustration from a magazine.

Figure 19. Replica of an Italian style leather and wood grip.

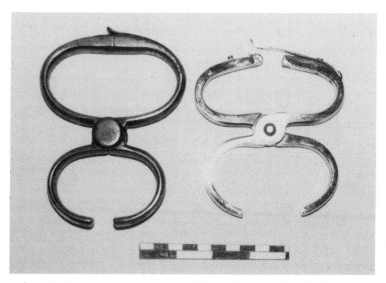

Figure 20. Standard grips, Pape's of about 1900 and Clejuso's of about 1990.

Figure 21. "Plug Eight" handcuffs, showing the plug removed for unlocking. (C.G.Coll.).

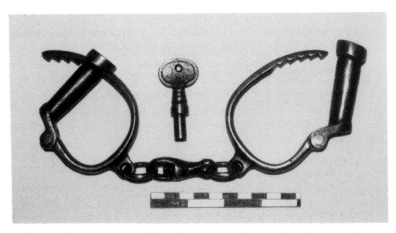

Figure 22. Reuben Craddock & Sons "Scotland Yard" pattern adjustable handcuffs.

34

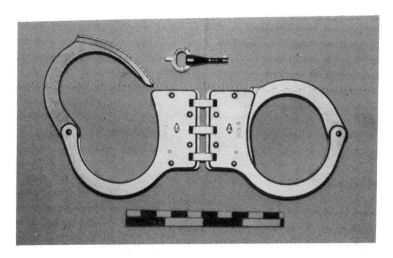

Figure 23. American Handcuff Co. hinged handcuffs model N-100.

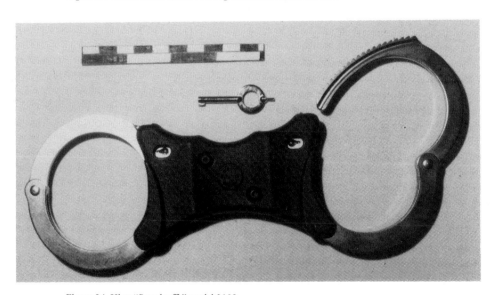

Figure 24. Hiatt "Speedcuffs" model 2103.

35

Figure 25. Harrington & Richardson "Super" or "F.B.I." model 123.

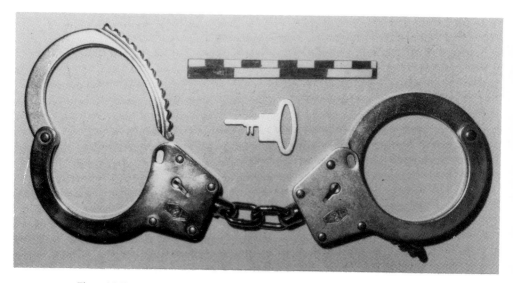

Figure 26. Bren (Pouta) handcuffs. Note the key.

Figure 27. Chubb "Escort" handcuffs, adjustable to three sizes of wrist. Note the inserts for use on very small wrists.

Figure 28. Australian Defence Industries "Saf-Lok-Mark-IV" handcuffs.

Figure 29. Rivolier high security model handcuffs. Note two different keys.

Figure 30. Clejuso heavyweight model 15 handcuffs. Weight 1.3 kg. (2lb.10oz.).

Figure 31. Hiatt standard pattern leg-irons.

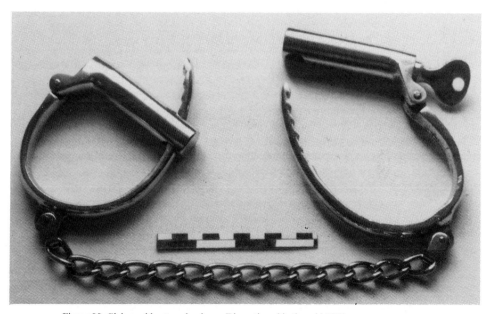

Figure 32. Clejuso old pattern leg-irons. Discontinued in the mid 1980s.

Figure 33. Smith & Wesson model 110 leg-irons, with short linkage for use as large handcuffs.

Figure 34. Clejuso new pattern leg-irons.

40

Figure 35. Rivolier leg-irons.

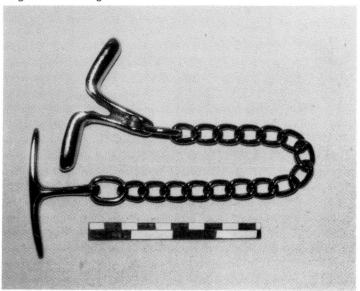

Figure 36. Clejuso steel chain "Wrist crackers" grip.

41

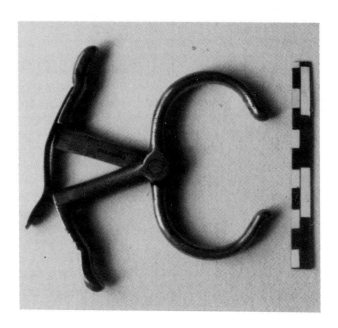

Figure 37. Phillips "Nipper" grip.

Figure 38. Taiwanese "Claw" grip.

42

Figure 39. German "Claw" grip.

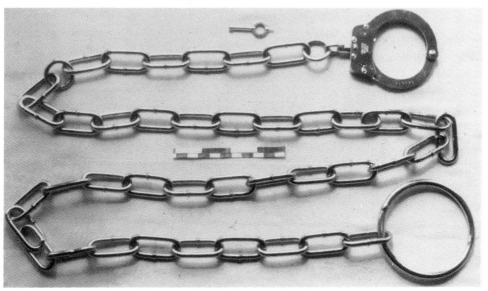

Figure 40. Hiatt-Thompson model 6010 single shackle and leading chain.

43

Figure 41. Prisoner in the American Handcuff Company model L-300 "Auto Restraint" combination set.

Figure 42. Smith & Wesson model 1800 belly chain handcuffs. (See also back cover).

Figure 43. Prisoner in a replica Prison Department restraint belt.

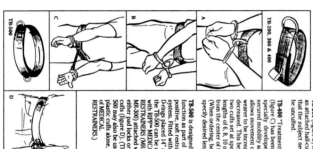

RIPP™ TRANSPORT BELTS are made from 2" wide, 1400 LB polypropylene webbed belt and hook & loop materials. The method of closure provides a double seal for strength and security, and it allows the size to expand from a 20" to 48" waist. (May also be ordered in XL sizes to fit up to 60" waists.)

TB-200 (figure A) is fitted with a 2" wide steel D-ring for use with any set of standard handcuffs.

TB-300 (figure B) features an attached half-cuff so that the subject need never be uncuffed.

TB-400 "Treatment Belt" (figure C) has been specially developed for secured mobility and allows movement of the wearer to be increased or decreased. This belt has two cuffs set at specified lengths of 6, 8, 10 or 12" from the center of the belt. (When ordering, be sure to specify desired length.)

TB-500 is designed to function as part of a positive, soft restraint system. Fitted with two 1" D-rings placed 14" apart, the TB-500 can be used with RIPP™ MEDICAL RESTRAINERS (MR-100 or MR-300) attached with either pad locks or plastic cuffs (figure D). (The TB-500 may also be used with plastic cuffs alone, instead of MEDICAL RESTRAINERS.)

Figure 44. RIPP "D-ring" belt   (RIPP catalogue illustration).

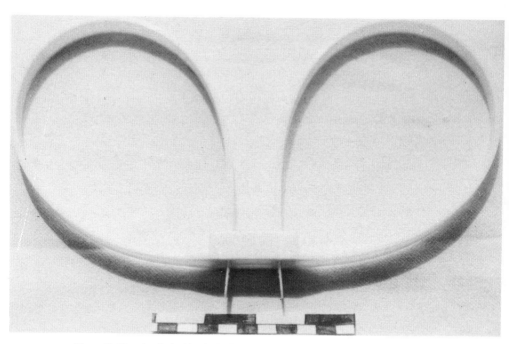

Figure 45. Monadnock double plasticuffs.

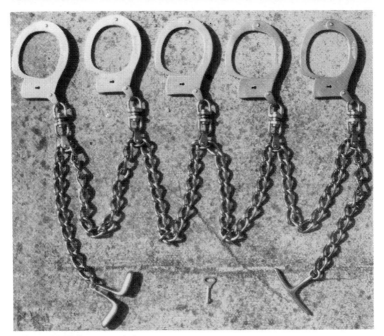

Figure 46. Clejuso gang chain.

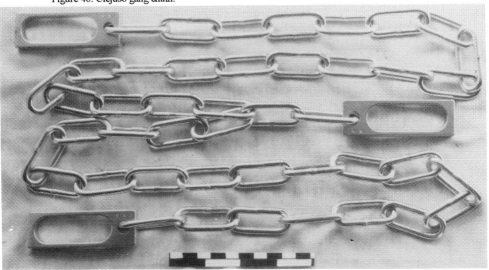

Figure 47. C & S Security Company gang chain. This one has three security links, but can be manufactured to have as many links as the customer requires.

47

Figure 48. Taiwanese thumbcuffs.

Figure 49. Various toy handcuffs.

48